D1318263

DATE DUE

JA 3 0			

220.5   **Volume 5**
Ch   The Children's Bible. [The world's
         greatest stories illustrated in full
         color] [12 volume set] N.Y., A Golden
         Press/Funk & Wagnalls, Inc., c.1965,1981.
         765p.   illus.

         ISBN:0-8343-0037-0

         1.Bible.

THE CHILDREN'S BIBLE

Volume 5

A Golden Press / Funk & Wagnalls, Inc. Book

Published by Western Publishing Company, Inc.

COPYRIGHT © 1981, 1965 BY WESTERN PUBLISHING COMPANY, INC. COPYRIGHT © 1962 BY FRATELLI FAB-BRI, MILAN, ALL RIGHTS RESERVED. PRINTED IN THE U.S.A. PUBLISHED BY GOLDEN PRESS, NEW YORK, BY ARRANGEMENT WITH WESTERN PUBLISHING—HACHETTE INTERNATIONAL, S.A., GENEVA. GOLDEN® AND GOLDEN PRESS® are trademarks of Western Publishing Company, Inc.

Classic™ binding
R. R. Donnelley & Sons Company
patents--U.S. pending

Distributed by Funk & Wagnalls, Inc. New York

Library of Congress Catalog Card Number: 81-81439

ISBN 0-8343-0042-7 (Volume 5)
ISBN 0-8343-0037-0 (12 Volume Set)

CONTENTS

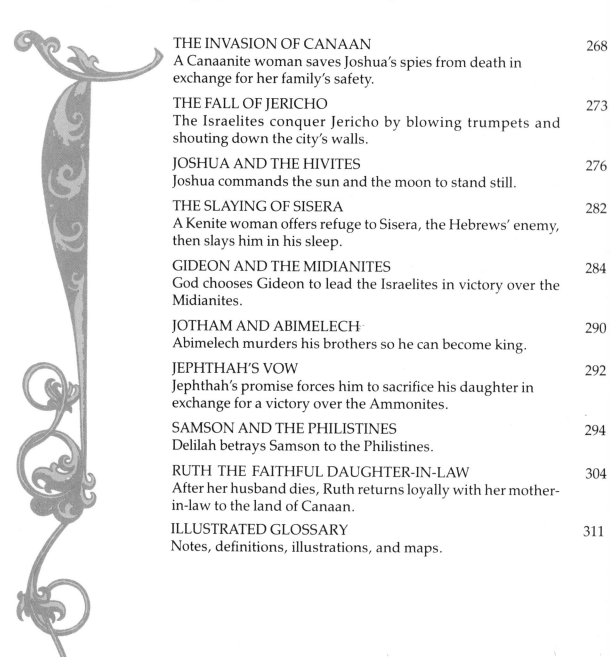

INTRODUCTION

After Moses' death, Joshua became the leader of the Israelites. Joshua was Moses' friend and helper during the years the Israelites wandered in the desert between Egypt and Canaan. Joshua was the only person Moses allowed to be with him when the Lord spoke to him. Moses taught Joshua to lead the army, and Moses relied on Joshua to help him during the desert battles that the Israelites fought against their enemies.

It was Joshua who finally led the children of Israel into the Promised Land. He was a smart and brave general. He also had great faith in God and obeyed God's commandments. The story of Joshua and the Israelite conquest of the land of Canaan is told in the Book of Joshua.

The Israelites probably entered the Promised Land around the year 1200 B.C. Other people were living there then. Some of these people were Hebrew people who had been living in the land of Canaan since the time of Abraham and Isaac and Jacob. These Hebrew people had not gone into Egypt during the great famine of Joseph's time. They welcomed the Israelites returning from Egypt. But the people of Canaan who were not Hebrews did not want the Israelites to live in their country. They tried to stop the Israelites, and the Israelites had to fight their way into Canaan.

The Israelites believed that God wanted them to live in Canaan. They remembered the promises that God had made to Abraham, Isaac, and Jacob. God had told these patriarchs that someday their people would live in the land of Canaan. The Israelites believed that God led their army into Canaan.

The Canaanites were a difficult foe to defeat because their cities were surrounded by thick walls to keep invaders out. These walls were so big that some people actually built their houses right into the city's walls. Rahab, the woman who helped the Israelites invade Jericho, had a house that was built into the city wall. The Canaanites also stored water in their cities so that their enemies could not cut off their water supply. With their strong walls and good water supply, the Canaanites thought their cities were safe from their enemies.

The Israelites carried the Ark of the Covenant with them into battle. The Ark was the golden box where they kept the two tablets of stone bearing God's commandments. When the Israelites saw the Ark, they became strong and fought well because they knew that God was with them. They were fierce warriors.

Joshua and the tribes of Israel defeated many kings in the land of Canaan. The Israelites captured big and important cities in the north and south of Canaan, but they did not take over the entire land of Canaan. They did not capture the coast, and they did not conquer the fortress at Jerusalem. The stronghold at Jerusalem remained in the hands of the Jebusites until it was captured later in Israel's history by King David.

After the Israelites had captured most of the land of Canaan, they divided it among the tribes that made up the people of Israel. Then the Israelites settled down on the land. They once again became farmers and shepherds. The land was good to them and they were prosperous. After their long years in the desert, the people were happy to live in Canaan. They were no longer slaves as they had been in Egypt.

The Twelve Tribes ruled the land of Canaan. Each tribe lived on its own land and took care of its own affairs. Each tribe was led by a patriarch, an old and wise man who gave advice to his people and settled their arguments. The people of Israel at this time did not have an army, so the tribes helped defend each other against their enemies. The stronger tribes protected the weaker ones. The Israelites' only defense against their enemies was for the tribes to join forces and fight side by side.

The tribes were bound together by the promise they had made to God at Mt. Sinai. This promise was called the covenant. The people of Israel had promised God that they would always obey his laws, and in turn God promised them that he would always guide and protect them. The Israelites tried to live according to the law of God. They tried to keep their part of the covenant.

Every year the leaders of the Twelve Tribes met together in the town of Shiloh. After the conquest of the Promised Land, the Ark of the Covenant was kept in Shiloh. The shrine in Shiloh was guarded by a high priest, who was helped by many other priests. The high priests of this shrine were the descendents of Aaron, Moses' brother, and were from the tribe of Levi.

The leaders of the Twelve Tribes came to Shiloh to show God that they were still faithful to him. The people of Israel also went to Shiloh once a year for a great religious celebration. During the celebration they thanked God for leading them out of Egypt, for feeding them, and for giving them water on their journey to Canaan. The people of Israel knew that they were living in the Promised Land only because God wanted them to live there. They offered sacrifices of animals to God to thank him for his help and protection. They promised God that they would always keep his law.

The people of Israel did not always keep their promise, however. As they grew prosperous they sometimes forgot that God had rescued them from the pharaohs. They forgot that God had given them the land of Canaan as their home. They even began to set up altars to other gods. Because they wanted good crops, they prayed to the Canaanite god Baal. The Canaanites believed that Baal gave them plentiful harvests. God became angry with his people when they worshipped other gods. He allowed other nations to attack and conquer some of the tribes of Israel. The Israelites had to do battle with other peoples who came into the Promised Land.

The Israelites had to defend themselves against the Philistines, who were their worst enemy. The Philistines lived to the south and west of the Promised Land. They were a powerful people who made their weapons and chariots out of iron. The Israelites made their weapons out of wood and stone. The Israelites also had to defend themselves against the Midianites. The Midianites were fierce nomads who came from the lands east of Israel. They swooped down on the Israelites on fast camels and terrified them. The Israelites had to defend themselves against many other invaders.

God never forgot his people, however, even when they had broken their promise to him. He never abandoned his people to their enemies, and he raised up heroes in Israel to lead the tribes against their enemies. These men and women were called judges. God made these men and women strong and clever, so they could defeat the enemies of Israel. The story of the judges is told in the Book of Judges. The events which are described in the Book of Judges took place between 1220 and 1050 B.C.

The judges did not always understand God. They did not always act in ways that God liked. Jephthah, for example, killed his daughter because of a promise he had made to God. Jephthah did not know that God hated human sacrifice. And Samson was fond of tricks and lies. Even though God did not like the way these people acted, he made them strong so that they could defend the Israelites. He blessed them so that they could help his people.

God never left his people during this hard time in their history. He punished them because they betrayed him, but he never let Israel be destroyed. The people owed their lives and the life of their nation to God. All God wanted in return was for them to keep his commandments. Jews and Christians today take great comfort from these stories of God's faithfulness and patience. They know that he will never abandon them and that he will always give them a chance to come back to him.

from the
BOOK OF JOSHUA

THE INVASION OF CANAAN

 FTER the death of Moses, the Lord put Joshua in command of the children of Israel. "Be strong and full of courage," said the Lord. "Do not be afraid, and do not be dismayed; for the Lord your God is with you wherever you go."

Joshua commanded the officers of the people: "Go among the people and tell them to prepare food, for within three days we shall cross Jordan River to enter the land which the Lord has given us."

He said this to all the people and they agreed to obey him as they had obeyed Moses.

JOSHUA SENDS SPIES

Joshua sent two men to spy on Jericho. They went there and came to the house of a woman named Rahab and took a room there.

But the king of Jericho was warned of their arrival and sent word to Rahab: "Bring out the men who came to you and are now in your house, for they have come to spy in our country."

But the woman took the two men and hid them, and when questioned, she replied: "There were two men who came here, but I did not know where they had come from. And the men left about the time it was getting dark. Where they were going I do not know, but if you pursue them quickly you will overtake them."

The woman had taken the spies up

on to the roof of her house and had hidden them under stalks of flax which she had laid out on the roof.

And the men searched for them all the way to the Jordan River.

Before the men on the roof had lain down for the night Rahab came up to them and said: "I know that the Lord has given you this land, and that all its inhabitants are afraid of you. For we have heard how the Lord dried up the waters of the Red Sea for you when you came out of Egypt, and as soon as we heard that, our hearts melted, and not a man had any courage left, all because of you. For the Lord your God is God in heaven above and in the earth beneath. Therefore I pray you, swear to me by the Lord, that since I have shown you kindness you will show kindness to me and my family. Promise to save the lives of my father and my mother and my brothers and sisters, and all their possessions, and make sure that we are not killed."

THE SPIES MAKE A PROMISE

The men said: "We will save your lives in exchange for our own, on the condition that you do not utter a word about us to the king. And when the Lord has given us this land, we will deal kindly and honestly with you."

Rahab's house was built upon the town wall, so she tied a rope to the parapet and the men climbed down it. As they went she said: "Go to the mountains and hide there for three days until your pursuers have come back here; and after that you may go on your way."

anyone goes out from your house into the street, whatever happens to him will be his own fault, and we shall not be guilty; but we will be responsible for whom ever stays with you in the house, and we will see that no one touches him. But if you say a word about our business here, then we will not keep our promise."

"It shall be just as you say," she said. Then she sent them away, and after they had left she tied the piece of scarlet cord in the window.

The two men went into the mountains and stayed there for three days while the pursuers searched unsuccessfully for them, and finally gave up the hunt and went back to the city.

And the men said: "We shall keep this oath which you have made us swear. When the children of Israel come into the land, you must tie a piece of scarlet cord in the window, and bring your father and mother and your brothers and all your father's household into your house. Then if

Then the two men came back down the mountain and crossed the river and came back to Joshua. They told him all the things that had happened to them. And they said to Joshua: "Truly the Lord has delivered all the country into our hands, for all the people of Jericho faint with fear of us."

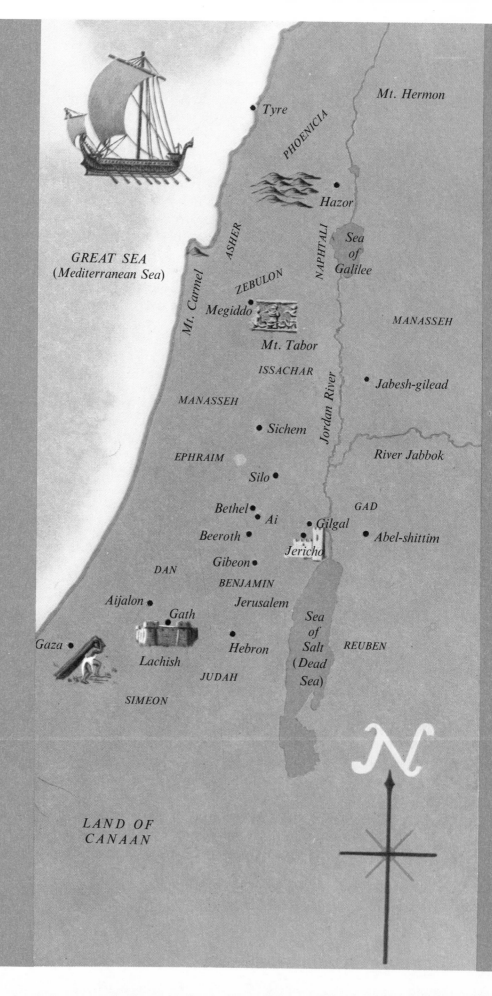

THE FALL OF JERICHO

JERICHO, that great city, was tightly shut up, because of the children of Israel; no one went out of the city, and no one came in.

Then the Lord told Joshua how he and the children of Israel could capture the city. Joshua called the priests and the people and gave them their orders.

To the priests he said: "Take up the ark of the covenant and let seven priests carrying seven trumpets of rams' horns march before the ark of the Lord." And to the people he said: "Surround the city, and let those that are armed march before the ark of the Lord."

When Joshua had spoken to the people, the seven priests bearing seven trumpets of rams' horns went forward before the ark of the Lord and blew on their trumpets. The armed men went before the priests and the rear guard followed after the ark of the Lord.

Joshua had commanded the people: "You shall not shout nor make any noise nor shall any word come out of your mouths until the day when I bid you shout. Then you shall shout."

So the ark of the Lord circled the city, going about it once. Then everyone came back to the camp and stayed there.

Next day Joshua rose early in the morning, and the priests took up the ark of the Lord. Again seven priests, bearing seven trumpets of rams' horns, went steadily ahead, blowing on their trumpets. The armed guard went before them, and the rear guard came after the ark of the Lord.

The second day they circled the city once and returned to the camp. This they did for six days.

On the seventh day they rose early, at the dawning of the day, and circled the city in the same way seven times.

At the seventh time, while the priests blew on their trumpets, Joshua said to the people: "Shout, for the Lord has given you the city. And the city and everyone in it shall be accursed, except for Rahab, who shall live, she and all that are with her in the house, because she hid the messengers that we sent."

So the people shouted while the priests blew on their trumpets. When the people heard the sound of the trumpet and shouted with a great shout, the wall of Jericho fell down flat. The people of Israel went into the city, each man walking straight ahead, and they took the city and put all its inhabitants to the sword.

RAHAB IS SPARED

But Joshua had said to the two men who had spied for him: "Go into Rahab's house and bring out the woman and all her family, as you promised her."

And the young men who had served as spies went in and brought out Rahab and her father and her mother and her brothers and all their possessions. They brought out all her family and left them outside the city at the camp of the Israelites.

Then they burned the city and all that was in it, except for the silver and gold and the vessels of brass and iron, which they put into the treasury of the house of the Lord.

And Joshua saved Rahab's life and her father's household and all that she had, and she went to live in Israel. He did this because she had hidden the messengers he had sent to spy on the city of Jericho.

275

JOSHUA
AND THE
HIVITES

ND God said to Joshua: "Fear not, and be not dismayed. Take all the people of war with you and go up to the city of Ai. I have given to you the king of Ai and his people and his city and his land, and you shall do to Ai and her king as you did to Jericho and her king."

So Joshua did as the Lord had told him. He ambushed the city of Ai and destroyed it utterly. And the possessions and the cattle of the people of Ai were given as booty to the children of Israel.

All the cities of Jordan were afraid of Joshua when they heard what had happened to Jericho and Ai. And they gathered themselves together with one accord to fight with Joshua and Israel.

The people of Gibeon, who were

rich and wily, wanted to make a treaty with him. They sent messengers, dressed in tattered clothing, with mouldy bread in their packs and with patched and leaking wineskins. These messengers came to Joshua in his camp at Gilgal, saying that they had come from a far country.

But Joshua said: "Who are you? And where do you come from?"

The men of Gibeon answered: "We have come from a very distant country. This bread of ours was taken hot and fresh from the oven when we started out, and now, behold, it is dry and mouldy. These skins which we filled with wine were then new, and, behold, they are split. And our garments and shoes have become old because of the length of our journey."

The men of Israel looked at the food and the wineskins and the clothes and did not ask counsel from the mouth of the Lord. Joshua drew up a peace treaty and swore a solemn oath that the Israelites would keep it.

But three days later they learned that these were their neighbors, the Hivites. The children of Israel reached the rich city of Gibeon, but they could not fight, because of the solemn peace treaty.

Then Joshua sent for the Hivites and asked: "Why have you cheated us, saying you live very far from us, when you dwell among us? Now you are cursed, and none of you shall be freed from being bondsmen and hewers of wood and drawers of water for the house of God."

And the people of Gibeon said: "We were told that the Lord your God commanded his servant Moses to give you all the land and to destroy all the inhabitants of the land. Therefore we were afraid of our lives, because of you, and that is why we did this thing. But now we are in your hands and we shall do as you say."

THE SUN AND MOON
OBEY JOSHUA

When the king of Jerusalem heard that Joshua had made peace with the Hivites he was afraid, because Gibeon was a rich and royal city and its men were famous for their might. So he conspired with four other kings and they set forth to lay siege to Gibeon.

The Gibeonites sent a message to Joshua, who was in his camp at Gilgal, saying: "Come quickly and save us, for all the kings of the Amorites that dwell in the mountains have joined together against us."

And God said unto Joshua: "Fear them not, for I have delivered them into your hands. Not a man of them shall stand before thee."

So Joshua and his army left Gilgal and took the Amorites by surprise and killed many of them and put the others to flight. As they fled, the Lord cast hailstones from heaven upon them, and more Amorites died from these hailstones than were killed by the children of Israel.

Then Joshua spoke: "Sun, stand still above Gibeon, and moon, stay above the valley of Ajalon."

And the sun stood still and the moon stayed, until the Israelites had avenged themselves upon their enemies. And never before had there been a day like this, when the Lord obeyed the voice of a man; for the Lord fought for Israel.

So Joshua struck all the country of the hills and of the vale and of the springs, and all their kings. He left none remaining, but utterly destroyed all that breathed, as the Lord God of Israel commanded. All these kings and their land did Joshua take, because the Lord God of Israel fought for Israel.

Joshua made war a long time. There was not a city that made peace with the children of Israel, except the Hivites,

the inhabitants of Gibeon. All others they took in battle. So Joshua took the whole land, according to all that the Lord said to Moses, and Joshua gave it for an inheritance to Israel, according to their division by tribes. And the land rested from war.

THE AGED JOSHUA SPEAKS
TO THE PEOPLE

And it came to pass, a long time after the Lord had given Israel rest from all their enemies round about, that Joshua waxed old and stricken in age.

So he called for all Israel, and for their elders, and for their heads, and for their judges, and for their officers, and said to them:

"I am old and stricken in age. And you have seen all that the Lord your

God has done to these nations because of you. Behold, I have divided among you by lot these nations that remain, to be an inheritance for your tribes. And the Lord your God, he shall expel them from before you and drive them from out of your sight, and you shall possess their land, as the Lord your God has promised you.

"Be you therefore very courageous to do all that is written in the book of the law of Moses, and turn not aside, either to the right or the left. Of these nations that remain among you, neither make mention of the name of their gods nor swear by them nor serve them nor bow down to them. Take care that you love the Lord your God. Otherwise, if you do associate with the survivors of these nations, know for a certainty that the Lord will no longer drive out any nations from before you, but they shall be snares and traps to you, and scourges in your sides, and thorns in your eyes; until you perish from this good land which the Lord has given you.

"And, behold, this day I am going to die. And you know in your hearts and in your souls that not one thing has failed of all the good things which the Lord your God spoke concerning you. All have come to pass, and not one thing has failed."

So Joshua let the people depart, every man to his inheritance. And it came to pass after these things that Joshua, the son of Nun, the servant of the Lord, died, being a hundred and ten years old. And they buried him in the borders of his inheritance, in Timnath-serah which is on the mount of Ephraim, on the north side of the hill of Gaash.

from the
BOOK OF JUDGES

THE SLAYING OF SISERA

BECAUSE the children of Israel did evil in the sight of the Lord, the Lord made them the captives of Jabin, king of Canaan. Jabin's army was commanded by a great captain called Sisera. He had nine hundred chariots, and for twenty years he oppressed the children of Israel.

One of the judges in Israel was a woman called Deborah, and she sent for a man called Barak and said: "Go to Mount Tabor with ten thousand men and I will deliver Sisera with all his soldiers and his chariots into your hands."

Barak said: "I will go if you accompany me, but not otherwise."

So Deborah agreed to go with him, but she warned him that he would gain no honor from the expedition, for the Lord would sell Sisera into the hands of a woman.

The armies of Barak and Sisera met on the slopes of Mount Tabor and the Lord defeated Sisera and his chariots, and Barak slew all his men. Sisera himself alighted from his chariot and fled on foot. When he reached Kedesh he stopped at the tent of Heber the Kenite, who was one of his king's allies. Heber's wife, Jael, came out to meet him, saying: "Come in, do not be afraid."

Sisera went into the tent, and Jael made him lie down and covered him with a cloak.

He said: "I am thirsty, give me some water to drink."

She gave him milk to quench his thirst and made him comfortable. He said: "Stand in the door of the tent, and if anybody comes and asks any questions, say that there is nobody here." Then Sisera fell asleep, for he was very tired, and while he slept Jael killed him.

Presently Barak appeared in pursuit of Sisera, and Jael went up to him and said: "Come and I will show you the man for whom you are looking."

So the children of Israel conquered Jabin, king of Canaan, and the land was at peace for forty years.

SONG OF REJOICING

Then Deborah and Barak the son of Abinoam sang on that day these words:

Praise ye the Lord
  for the avenging of Israel,
When the people willingly offered themselves.
Hear, O ye kings; give ear, O ye princes.
I, even I, will sing unto the Lord;
I will sing praise to the Lord God of Israel.
Lord, when thou wentest out of Seir,
When thou marchedst
  out of the field of Edom,
The earth trembled, and the heavens dropped,
The clouds also dropped water.
The mountains melted from before the Lord,
Even that Sinai
  from before the Lord God of Israel.
Blessed above women shall Jael
  the wife of Heber the Kenite be;
Blessed shall she be above women in the tent.
He asked water, and she gave him milk.
She brought forth butter in a lordly dish.
She put her hand to the nail,
And her right hand to the workman's hammer,
And with the hammer she smote Sisera,
  she smote off his head,
When she had pierced
  and stricken through his temples
At her feet he bowed, he fell, he lay down.
Where he bowed, there he fell down dead.
So let all your enemies perish, O Lord.

GIDEON AND THE MIDIANITES

IN time the children of Israel went back to their evil ways. Because of this the Lord delivered them into the power of the Midianites for seven years. The Midianites ravaged the land, and the children of Israel were obliged to live in dens in the mountains and in caves and fortified places.

When the seven years were up, an angel of the Lord came and sat under an oak in Ophrah which belonged to Joash the Abiezerite. His son Gideon was threshing wheat to hide from the Midianites.

AN ANGEL APPEARS TO GIDEON

The angel of the Lord appeared to Gideon and said to him: "The Lord is with you, you mighty man of valor."

Gideon said to him: "O my Lord, if the Lord is with us, why has all this happened to us? Where are all his miracles, of which our fathers told us? Did not the Lord bring us up from Egypt? The Lord has forsaken us now, and has given us up to the Midianites."

The angel looked at him and said: "Go out in your strength and you shall save Israel from the Midianites. Have I not sent you?"

"If I have found favor in your sight," Gideon said to him, "show me a sign that it it is you who are talking with me. Stay here until I come back and bring a present and set it before you."

"I will wait here until you come again," the angel said.

So Gideon went in and prepared a young goat and some unleavened cakes. The meat he put in a basket and he put the broth in a pot and brought it out to the angel and presented it.

The angel of God said to him: "Take the meat and the unleavened cakes and lay them upon this rock and pour out the broth."

Gideon did as he was commanded. Then the angel of the Lord stretched out the end of the staff that was in his hand and touched the meat and the unleavened cakes, and fire rose up out of the rock and consumed the meat and the unleavened cakes. And the angel of the Lord disappeared from sight.

When Gideon saw that this was indeed an angel of the Lord, he said: "Alas! O Lord God! I am frightened because I have seen an angel of the Lord God face to face."

But God said to him: "Be at peace, do not be afraid, you shall not die."

Then Gideon built an altar to the Lord and called it Yahweh-Shalom, which means "The Lord is Peace."

GOD ADDRESSES GIDEON

That same night God spoke to him again and said: "Take a seven-year-old bull from your father's herd, and go to the altar which your father has set up to Baal. Throw down the altar and cut down the grove of trees that is by it. Then build an altar to the Lord God on the top of the rock, and kindle a fire from the wood of the grove, and sacrifice the bull to the Lord."

So Gideon took ten of his servants and did as the Lord had commanded him to do. He dared not do it in the daytime, for fear of the villagers and the rest of his father's household, so he did it under cover of night.

The next morning the villagers saw what had happened. When they discovered that Gideon was responsible for the pulling down of Baal's altar, they went to Joash and said: "Bring out your son, for he must die."

But Joash defended Gideon and said: "Do you have to plead for Baal, who is a god? If any of you dare to, let him be put to death at once. Let Baal speak for himself."

Then the Midianites and the Amalekites banded together and camped in the valley of Jezreel, but the spirit of the Lord came upon Gideon and he blew a trumpet and all the men flocked to his side.

Gideon spoke to the Lord saying: "If you will save Israel by my hand, give me a token. Behold, I shall put a fleece of wool on the floor and if the dew is on the fleece only and all the earth beside it is dry, I shall know that you mean me to save Israel."

The next morning he rose early and wrung a bowlful of water out of the fleece.

But still he doubted and said: "Do not be angry with me, but grant me one more sign. Let the fleece be dry and upon all the ground let there be dew." And the Lord did so that night; for only the fleece was dry, and there was dew on all the ground.

GIDEON PICKS HIS MEN

Then Gideon assembled an army of the men of Israel behind him. They pitched their tents beside the well of Harod, so that the ranks of the Midianites were off to the north of them by the hill of Moreh, in the valley.

And God said to Gideon: "The people with you are too many for me to give them a victory over the Midianites, for then Israel might boast of its own power, saying, 'Our own hands have saved us.' Go to the people, therefore, and tell everyone who is fearful and afraid, to go back, and leave Mount Gilead."

Twenty-two thousand of the people returned, and ten thousand stayed.

Then God spoke to Gideon, saying: "There are still too many people. Bring them down to the water, and I will test them for you. If I say, 'This one shall go with you,' he shall go with you, and if I say, 'This one shall not go with you,' he shall not go."

So Gideon brought the people down to the water, and God said to Gideon: "Set apart those who lap the water with their tongues, as a dog laps, and those who kneel down to drink."

The number of those who lapped, putting their hands to their mouths, was three hundred men. All the rest of the people bowed down upon their knees to drink the water.

Then God said to Gideon: "By the three hundred men who lapped, I will save you and will deliver the Midianites into your hands. Let all the other people go to their homes."

So the chosen people took food in their hands, and their trumpets, and Gideon sent all the rest of the Israelites to their tents and kept only those three hundred men. And the army of Midian was beneath, in the valley.

THEY SPY ON THE MIDIANITES

The same night God spoke to Gideon, saying:

"Arise, go down to the camp, for I have given it into your hands. But if you are afraid to go down, take your servant Phurah down with you to the camp. You will hear what the Midianites are saying, and afterward your hands will be strengthened for the battle."

Gideon went down with Phurah to the outermost of the armed men that

were in the camp. There the Midianites and the Amalekites and all the children of the east lay along the valley, like grasshoppers in their numbers, and their camels were countless, as many as the sands by the seaside.

When Gideon came near, a man was telling a dream to his companion, and he said:

"I have dreamed a dream, and in it a cake of barley bread tumbled into the camp of Midian. It came to a tent and struck it so that the tent fell and overturned, and lay upon the ground."

His companion answered and said: "This is nothing else than the sword of Gideon, the son of Joash, a man of Israel. For God is giving him a victory over Midian and all the army."

When Gideon heard the telling of the dream and the interpretation of it, he worshiped God. Then he returned to the army of Israel and said: "Arise, for the Lord has given into your hands the army of Midian."

He divided the three hundred men into three companies, and he put a trumpet into every man's hand, and gave them empty pitchers with lights inside them.

"Watch me and do likewise," he said to them. "And see that when I come to the outskirts of the camp, you do whatever I do. When I and those who are with me blow on our trumpets, then you blow on your trumpets too, on every side of the whole camp, and shout: 'The sword of the Lord and of Gideon!'"

THE ISRAELITES ATTACK

So Gideon and the hundred men who were with him came to the outskirts of the camp in the beginning of the middle watch, when a new watch had just been posted. Then they blew on their trumpets and broke the pitchers that they held in their hands. And the three companies all blew on their trumpets and broke the pitchers and held the lights in their left hands and the trumpets in their right hands. And they cried: "The sword of the Lord and of Gideon!"

They stood, every man in his place, round about the camp, and all the army of Midian awoke and cried out.

The three hundred blew on their trumpets and through the whole army of the Midianites the Lord made men turn their swords against one another, and they fled in confusion. The men of Israel pursued them beyond Jordan, killing their leaders Oreb and Zeeb.

Then the men of Israel said to Gideon: "Be our ruler, you and your son and your son's son, for you have delivered us from the hand of Midian."

But Gideon said: "I will not rule over you, neither shall my son rule over you. The Lord shall rule over you. But I have one request to make of you. Will you all give me the gold earrings that you took from your prey?"

For the Midianites were Ishmaelites and wore gold rings in their ears.

The men of Israel said: "We give them willingly."

They spread a cloak on the ground and every man cast in the earrings that he had taken from his victims. The weight of the earrings amounted to seventeen hundred shekels of gold, and there were also ornaments and collars and purple raiment from the kings of Midian, and the chains which had been round their camels' necks. And Gideon took all these and put them in his city of Ophrah.

Thus was Midian utterly conquered by the children of Israel, and the country lived in peace for forty years, during the life of Gideon.

JOTHAM
AND
ABIMELECH

GIDEON'S wives were many, and when he died he left seventy sons. One of these, Abimelech, went to his mother's people in Shechem and said to them: "Do you want all those seventy sons of Gideon to reign over you? Would you not rather it were I alone, who am your near relation?"

They agreed that they would rather have him as ruler, and they gave him seventy pieces of silver with which he hired mercenaries who followed him to Ophrah. There Abimelech slew all his brothers except Jotham, the youngest, who hid himself.

Then all the men of Shechem gathered together and hailed Abimelech as king.

Jotham heard of this and he went and stood on the top of Mount Gerizim, and lifted up his voice. And he cried: "Listen to me, you men of Shechem, that the Lord may give ear to you.

"The trees went forth once upon a time to choose a king, and they said to the olive tree, 'Rule over us.'

"But the olive tree said to them, 'Should I leave my rich oil, by means of which both men and gods are honored, and go to be king over the trees?'

"Then the trees said to the fig tree, 'You come and rule over us'.

"But the fig tree said to them, 'Should I forsake my sweetness and my good fruit, and go to be king over the trees?'

"Then the trees said to the vine, 'You come and rule over us.'

"And the vine said to them, 'Should I leave my wine which cheers gods and men, and go to be king over the trees?'

"Then all the trees said to the bramble, 'You come and rule over us.'

"And the bramble said: 'If you really appoint me king over you, then come and put your trust in my shadow, and if not, let fire come out of the bramble, and devour the cedars of Lebanon.'"

Jotham went on: "My father fought for you and risked his life and delivered you out of the hand of Midian. Today you have risen against my father's house and have slain his sons, and made Abimelech, the son of his maidservant, king, because he is your relation. If you consider that you dealt justly with Gideon, rejoice in Abimelech, and he in you, but if not, let Shechem destroy Abimelech, and let Abimelech devour Shechem."

Then Jotham ran away and he went to live in Beer, for fear of his brother Abimelech.

After three years Abimelech quarrelled with the men of Shechem who had raised him to power, and Abimelech destroyed them. But as he was besieging a tower within the city of Thebez, a woman cast a millstone down on his head.

Then Abimelech called his armor-bearer and said to him:

"Draw your sword and kill me, so that nobody can say that I was slain by a woman."

Thus was Jotham's parable fulfilled.

JEPHTHAH'S VOW

JEPHTHAH, the son of Gilead, was a mighty man of valor. He was a soldier of fortune who had been cast off by his brothers and therefore lived apart from them in the land of Tob. When the Ammonites made war against Israel, the people turned to Jephthah and asked him to be their captain and lead their armies.

This Jephthah agreed to do, but before going into battle he made a vow to the Lord. He said: "O God, if without fail you will deliver the children of Ammon into my hand, then when I return in peace to my own home, I swear that I shall offer up to the Lord as a burnt offering whatsoever shall first come out of the door of my house to greet me."

Then Jephthah went forth to battle and the Lord delivered the Ammonites into his power. He smote them from Aroer to Minnith and the plain of the vineyards, and destroyed them utterly.

After the battle he went back to Mizpah and as he approached his house, his daughter came out to meet him with timbrels and dances. She was his only child and he loved her more than all things of the world.

When he saw her Jephthah rent his garments and cried out in despair: "Alas, my daughter, what have you done to me? For I have pledged my word to the Lord and I cannot go back on it."

And he told her what he had done. His daughter answered:

"No, Father, you cannot break your

292

oath, since the Lord has given you the victory over the Ammonites. You must do unto me as you promised. But grant me one favor, let me live for two months, that I may go with my maids and weep over my youth and mourn for the children that will never be mine."

"Go," said her father.

So Jephthah's daughter and her maidens went into the mountains, and all together they bewailed her sad fate.

But when the two months were up she came back to her father's house and he fulfilled his oath and offered her up as a sacrifice to the Lord.

293

SAMSON AND THE PHILISTINES

FOR forty years the people of Israel were enslaved by the Philistines because of their evil ways in the sight of the Lord.

There was a man called Manoah of the family of the Danites, and he had no children. The angel of the Lord appeared to his wife and told her that she was to have a son.

The angel said: "Be cautious and drink no wine nor any strong drink, and do not eat any unclean thing. You will have a son and no razor shall come near his head, for he is dedicated to God from birth, and he shall begin to deliver Israel from the Philistines."

Later the angel appeared to Manoah also, and in due course he and his wife had a son whom they called Samson.

Samson grew up tall and strong, and when he was a grown man he went down to Timnath and saw a daughter of the Philistines and wanted to make her his wife. At first his parents withheld their accord, for they wished him to marry one of his own people. They did not know that this marriage was part of the Lord's plans to destroy the Philistines, but when Samson insisted, they abided by his wishes.

So Samson went to Timnath with his parents. As he came to the vineyards a young lion tried to attack him, and he killed it with his bare hands, but he did not tell his father and mother what he had done. He met the Philistine girl and spoke to her and she pleased him very much. When he returned again to see her, he turned aside to look for the carcass of the lion which he had killed, and found it with a swarm of bees and honey inside. He took out a handful of the honey and ate it, and gave some to his parents, but he did not tell them from where it came.

SAMSON'S RIDDLE

Later on, the marriage was arranged and a wedding feast was prepared. Thirty young Philistine men were present, and Samson said to them: "Here is a riddle for you, and if you can solve it for me within seven days of the feast, then I shall give you thirty sheets and thirty suits of clothes, but if you fail to find the answer, you must give me thirty sheets and thirty changes of clothing."

So they said: "Tell us your riddle."

Samson said: "Out of the eater came forth meat, and out of the strong came forth sweetness."

Three days passed and the Philistines had found no answer to the riddle.

On the seventh day they said to Samson's wife: "Coax your husband and persuade him to tell us the solution. Otherwise we shall set fire to your father's house and burn you alive."

Samson's wife wept and said to him: "You must hate me instead of loving me, for you have given my people a riddle to solve, and you have not told me the answer to it."

He said: "I have told neither my father nor my mother. Why should I tell you?"

She went on weeping for seven days all the time that their feast was going on. At last, on the seventh day, Samson could bear it no longer and he told her the answer and she passed it on to her countrymen.

Before sunset on the seventh day, the men of the city said to Samson: "What is sweeter than honey? And what is stronger than a lion?"

Samson saw what had happened and he said:

"You would never have found the answer to my riddle if you had not threatened my wife."

He went down to Ashkelon and there he killed thirty men and took their belongings. From these he took thirty suits of clothes, which he gave to the men who had answered the riddle. Then he went back to his father's house. He was exceedingly angry at the Philistines and with the woman whom he had married.

SAMSON ANGERS
THE PHILISTINES

He caught three hundred foxes and tied them tail to tail, and fixed torches between their tails. Then he set fire to the torches and let go the foxes to run among the cornfields of the Philistines. The shocks and the standing corn, the vineyards, and the olives all caught fire and were burned up.

After this the Philistines went up and pitched their camp in Judah at Lehi, and the men of Judah asked them why they had come.

The Philistines said: "We have come to capture and punish Samson."

Then three thousand men of Judah went up to the top of the rock Etam and said to Samson: "Do you not know that the Philistines are our overlords? We are going to bind you and give you into their hands."

Samson said: "Promise me that you will not yourselves attack me."

They said: "No, but we will bind you fast and hand you over to them. But we promise not to kill you."

So they bound him with two new cords and brought him up from the rock.

When he came to Lehi, where the Philistines were encamped, they shouted with triumph. But the spirit of the Lord descended upon Samson and the cords on his arms became as soft as scorched flax, and the fetters fell from his hands. He looked around and saw the clean white jawbone of an ass, and he picked it up, and with it he slew a thousand men.

Then he threw away the jawbone and called the place Remathlehi in memory of his victory. But now he was parched with thirst, and he called on the Lord and said: "Lord, you have granted me this great victory, but must I now die of thirst and fall into the hands of the enemy?"

God touched a hollow place in the rock, and water gushed out of it, so that Samson could drink his fill until his strength returned to him.

After that he became a judge in Israel under the Philistines and he judged the people for twenty years.

SAMSON'S MIGHTY STRENGTH

Samson loved a woman whose name was Delilah. The leaders of the Philistines came to her and said: "Coax him and learn what gives him his great strength, and by what means we may triumph over him, so that we may bind him and humble him. For this we will give you, each of us, eleven hundred pieces of silver."

So Delilah said to Samson: "Tell me, I beg you, what gives you your great strength, and how you could be bound to be made helpless."

"If anyone bound me with seven green willow stems that had never been dried, I should be as weak as any other man," Samson said to her.

Then the leaders of the Philistines brought to her seven green willow stems which had not been dried, and she bound him with them.

Now there were men lying in wait, waiting with her in the room. And she said to Samson: "The Philistines are upon you, Samson!"

But Samson broke the stems as a strand of hemp is broken when it touches the fire. So the secret of his strength was not known.

Delilah said to Samson: "See, you have mocked me and told me lies. Now tell me, I beg you, with what could you be securely bound?"

And he said to her: "If they bind me fast with new ropes that have never been used, then I shall be as weak as any other man."

Delilah therefore took new ropes and bound him with them and said to him: "The Philistines are upon you, Samson!"

And again there were men lying in wait in the room. But Samson broke the ropes from his arms like a thread.

Delilah said again to Samson: "Up to now you have mocked me and told me lies. Tell me now with what you could really be bound."

And he said to her: "Weave the seven locks of my hair with the web of cloth on your loom."

She did so while he slept, and fastened it with the pin of the loom. Then she said to him: "The Philistines are upon you, Samson!"

But he waked out of his sleep and carried away the pin of the loom and the web of cloth.

SAMSON TELLS HIS SECRET

Then she said to him: "How can you say 'I love you' when you do not trust me in your heart? Three times now you have mocked me and have not told me what the secret of your great strength is."

She continued entreating him every day, and when she had urged him, so that his soul was vexed unto death, he told her all that was in his heart.

"A razor has never touched my head," he said to her, "for I have been consecrated to God, since before I was born. If I were shaved, my strength would go from me, and I would become weak and be like any other man."

When Delilah saw that he had told her the secret of his heart, she called again for the lords of the Philistines, saying: "Come up once more, for he has told me the secret of his heart." Then the lords of the Philistines came up to her, bringing the money in their hands.

Delilah made Samson go to sleep with his head on her knees. Then she

called for a man and had him shave off the seven locks of Samson's hair. By that she humbled him, for his strength went from him.

Then she said: "The Philistines are upon you, Samson!"

He awoke from his sleep and said: "I will go out, as I did the other times,

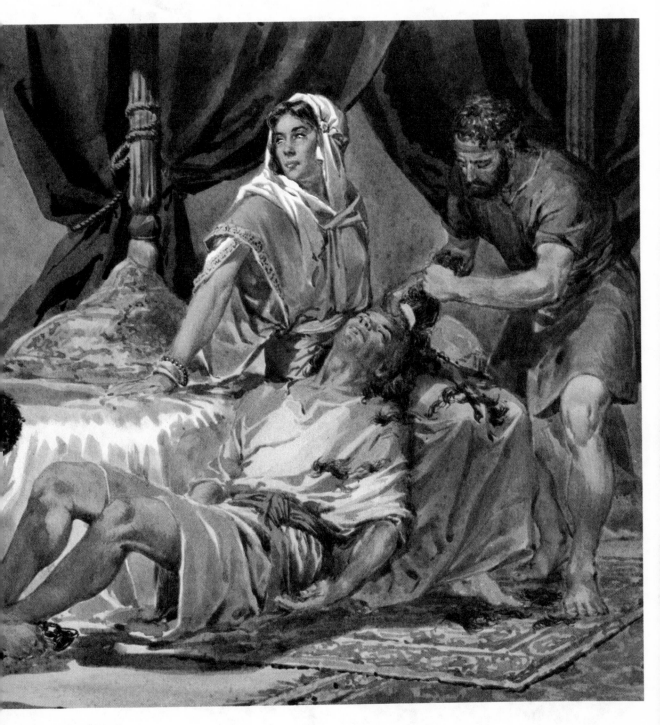

and shake myself." For he did not know that the power of the Lord was gone from him.

The Philistines quickly took him, and put out his eyes, and took him down to Gaza. There they bound him with fetters of brass and made him grind in the prison house.

SAMSON'S REVENGE

Gradually the hair of his head began to grow again. But the Philistines did not notice.

They gathered together to offer a great sacrifice to Dagon, their god, and to rejoice. They said: "Our god

has delivered Samson our enemy into our hands."

When they saw Samson they praised their god, for they said: "Our god has delivered into our hands our enemy and the destroyer of our country, who has slain many of us."

It happened that, while the hearts of the people were merry, they said: "Call Samson out, so that he can entertain us." So they brought Samson up out of the prison house and mocked him.

When they stood him up between two pillars, Samson said to the boy who held him by the hand:

"Let me feel the pillars which support the house, so that I may lean upon them."

Now the house was full of men and women, and all the leaders of the Philistines were there. There were about three thousand men and women on the roof, watching while Samson was being mocked.

Then Samson called out to the Lord and said:

"O Lord God, remember me, I pray you, and strengthen me, I pray you, only this once, O God, that I may take revenge on the Philistines for my two eyes."

Then Samson took hold of the two middle pillars upon which the house stood, and which held it up. He held one with his right hand, and the other with his left.

Samson said: "Let me die with the Philistines." And he bowed himself with all his might, and the house fell upon all the people who were inside. The number he killed at his death was greater than he killed in his life.

Then his brothers, and all the household of his father, came down and took his body. And they took him home, and buried him between Zorah and Eshtaol, in the burying place of Manoah his father.

from the
BOOK OF RUTH

RUTH
THE FAITHFUL
DAUGHTER-
IN-LAW

T happened, in the old days when the judges ruled Israel, that there was a famine in the land. And a certain man of Bethlehem of Judah went to stay in the country of Moab, he and his wife and his two sons. The name of the man was Elimelech, and the name of his wife was Naomi, and his two sons were Mahlon and Chilion. They came into the country of Moab and stayed there.

Elimelech, Naomi's husband, died, and she was left with her two sons. They took wives of the women of Moab. The name of the one was Orpah, and the name of the other, Ruth. They lived there for about ten years.

Then Mahlon and Chilion both died, and their mother was left without husband or sons. She arose with her daughters-in-law, to return home from the country of Moab, for she had heard in the country of Moab that the Lord had visited his people and given them food again. Therefore she left the place where she was, with her two daughters-in-law, and they started to go back to the land of Judah.

But Naomi said to her two daughters-in-law: "Go, return each of you to her mother's house. May the Lord be as kind to you as you have been to the dead and to me."

They lifted up their voices and wept. Orpah kissed her mother-in-law, but Ruth clung to her.

And Naomi said to Ruth: "See, your sister-in-law has gone back to her people and to her gods. You go after your sister-in-law."

But Ruth said: "Do not ask me to leave you or to go back instead of following after you. For where you go, I will go; and where you stop, I will stop. Your people shall be my people, and your God my God. Where you die, I shall die, and there will I be buried. The Lord punish me if anything but death part me from you!"

When Naomi saw that Ruth was determined to go with her, she agreed. So the two traveled on until they came to Bethlehem. They reached Bethlehem at the beginning of the barley harvest.

Now Naomi had a kinsman of her husband's, a mighty man of great wealth, of the family of Elimelech. His name was Boaz.

Ruth said to Naomi: "Let me go now to the fields and glean ears of grain after whoever gives me his permission to do so."

And Naomi said to her: "Go, my daughter."

So Ruth came to the field and gleaned after the reapers. It was her fortune to light on a part of the field belonging to Boaz.

RUTH PLEASES BOAZ

It happened that Boaz came from Bethlehem and said to the reapers: "The Lord be with you."

And they answered him: "The Lord bless you."

Then Boaz said to the servant who was in charge of the reapers: "Whose girl is that?"

The servant in charge of the reapers answered and said: "It is the Moabitish girl who came back with Naomi from the country of Moab. She asked permission to gather and glean after the reapers among the sheaves, so she came and has worked since morning, until just now when she rested a little in the shelter."

Then Boaz said to Ruth: "Do you hear me, my daughter? Do not go to glean in another field, nor go away from here, but stay close by my maid-servants. Watch the field where they reap and follow them. I have ordered the servants not to touch you. And when you are thirsty, go to the water jars and drink from the water which the young men have drawn."

Then she fell on her face and bowed herself to the ground and said to him: "Why should I have found favor in your eyes, that you should take notice of me, seeing that I am a stranger?"

Boaz answered and said to her: "I have heard all that you have done for your mother-in-law since the death of your husband, and how you have left your father and mother and the land of your birth, and have come to a people you had never known before. May the Lord repay your good deeds, and may a full reward be given you by the Lord God of Israel under whose wings you have come to rest."

Then she said: "Let me find favor in your sight, my lord; for you have comforted me by speaking friendly words to your handmaid, when I am not in truth a handmaid of yours."

And Boaz said to her: "At meal-time come here and eat of the bread and dip your piece into the sauce."

So she sat beside the reapers, and he passed her parched grain, and she ate until she had had enough, and then left.

When she arose to glean again, Boaz gave orders to his young men, saying: "Let her glean even among the sheaves, and do not reproach her. And also let fall some handfuls on purpose for her, and leave them so that she may glean them, and do not stop her."

So she gleaned in the field until evening, and threshed out what she had gleaned.

She gathered it up and went into the city and showed her mother-in-law what she had gleaned.

Her mother-in-law said to her: "Where did you glean today? Where did you work? Blessed be he that took notice of you."

She told her mother-in-law with whom she had worked, saying: "The man with whom I worked today is named Boaz."

Then Naomi said to her daughter-in-law: "May the Lord bless him, for the Lord has not stopped showing kindness to the living and the dead." And she added: "The man is near of kin to us, one of our next kinsmen."

Ruth said: "He told me, too, to stay near his young men until they have finished his harvest."

And Naomi said to Ruth: "It is good that you go out with his maid-servants, so that you do not go into any other field.

So Ruth stayed close to the maidens of Boaz to glean until the end of the barley harvest and of the wheat harvest; and she lived with her mother-in-law.

NAOMI INSTRUCTS RUTH

Then Naomi said to Ruth: "My daughter, I must seek peace that all may be well with you. Boaz, with whose maidens you have been working, is our kinsman and can help you. Tonight he is winnowing barley on the threshing floor. Wash and anoint yourself and put on your best robe and go down to the threshing floor and wait until he has finished eating and drinking. Then tell him you are there, and he will tell you what to do."

Ruth did all that her mother-in-law told her, and at midnight, after he had eaten and drunk, Boaz realized that she was there, and he said: "Who is it?"

She answered: "I am Ruth, your handmaid. Help me, for you are my near kinsman."

Boaz said: "The Lord bless you, my daughter, for you have proved yourself to be a virtuous woman, and I will do whatever you want. It is true that I am a near kinsman, but there is another who is even more closely related than I. Wait until tomorrow morning, and we shall see if he will perform his duty as your kinsman. If not, I swear before the Lord that I shall do it in his place. And now lie down until the morning."

So Ruth lay down on the threshing floor and the next morning Boaz said to her: "Bring your veil to me and hold it out."

When she did so he measured out six measures of barley into the veil, and she went back to the city and to her mother-in-law.

Ruth told Naomi all that Boaz had said and showed her the six measures of barley, and Naomi said: "Wait quietly, my daughter, until you know what is to result from this. This man will not rest until he has provided for you this very day."

In the meantime Boaz went up to the gate and there he met Ruth's kinsman and called him to stop and take counsel with him and with ten elders of the city.

Boaz said to the kinsman: "Naomi has returned from the land of Moab and is selling a piece of land which belonged to our brother Elimelech. I have thought to tell you of this in advance, so that you could buy it before the inhabitants and the elders of my people. If you wish to redeem it, do so. If not, tell me, so that I may know, for after you no man has the right to do so."

The kinsman said: "I will do so."

Then Boaz told him: "If you buy the land from Naomi, you must also marry Ruth the Moabitess, to raise up the name of the dead upon his inheritance."

When the kinsman heard this, he said: "I cannot redeem it for myself, for fear of risking my own inher-

itance. Will you take over my rights?"

It was the custom in Israel that if a man made over his rights, he took off his shoe and gave it to his neighbor. When the kinsman said to Boaz: "Buy it for yourself," he drew off his shoe. Boaz said to the elders and to all the people: "You are witnesses that I have bought from Naomi all that belonged to Elimelech, and to Chilion and Mahlon. And I have purchased Ruth the Moabitess, the wife of Mahlon, to be my wife, to raise up the name of the dead upon his inheritance. You are all witnesses."

And the elders and all the people agreed and said: "We are witnesses. And may the Lord bless your house and make it famous in Bethlehem."

So Boaz took Ruth as his wife and Ruth bore him a son. And the women said to Naomi: "Blessed be the name of the Lord, who has not left you without a kinsman, and may his name be famous in Israel. To you he shall be a restorer of your life and a support in your old age, for he is the child of your daughter-in-law who loves you and is better to you than seven sons."

So Naomi took the child and became his nurse.

And the women her neighbors said: "It is as though he were Naomi's own son."

And the child was called Obed. He became the father of Jesse, who was the father of David.

ILLUSTRATED
GLOSSARY

Ajalon (p. 278)

The valley of Ajalon was located in a hilly area called the Shephelah, west of the plain where the Philistines lived. The valley of Ajalon, like other valleys in the Shephelah, was wide and well-watered. It was famous for its fine crops of grain, grapes, and olives.

Ashkelon (p. 295)

Ashkelon was one of the five cities built by the Philistines. (See Philistines.) It was located on the coast and was a strong and well-defended city. Ashkelon was well known for its excellent fruits and vegetables.

Baal (p. 285)

Baal was the most important of the Canaanite gods. His name meant "Master," but Baal was also honored as "Lord of the Earth." The Canaanites paid him special honors as the god of the weather and of rich harvests. He was believed to rule the earth during the good growing season that lasted from May until September.

Local village gods were spoken of as "the Baals," meaning "the Masters."

Barley (p. 287)

Barley was an important grain crop to the people of Bible lands. It was easier to grow than wheat, surviving drier weather and growing on poorer soil. Barley was also less expensive than wheat. However, it was not as nutritious.

Much of the barley grown in biblical times was fed to cattle, but a quantity of it was also made into bread for the poor.

Evil ways (p. 284)

Some of the Hebrews forsook their Lord by worshipping the gods of the Amorites. These were the evil ways that so angered God.

Flax (p. 269)

Flax is the plant from which linen is made. Flax plants grow about three feet tall, and have light blue flowers. Linen is woven from the strong fibers in the plants' stems.

People in biblical lands made linen by beating the harvested plants to loosen the seeds and then drying the stems in the sun on their houses' flat roofs. The plants were soaked, dried again, and then combed to split the fibers, which were then spun, or twisted into threads that were ready to be woven into linen cloth.

Fleece (p. 285)

The single piece of wooly hair cut from one sheep is called a fleece. Fleece also means any amount of sheep's wool.

Gleaning (p. 304)

Picking over a field of wheat or barley after it had been reaped, to search for any remaining stalks, was called gleaning. When the reaping was finished, a farmer allowed the poor, who

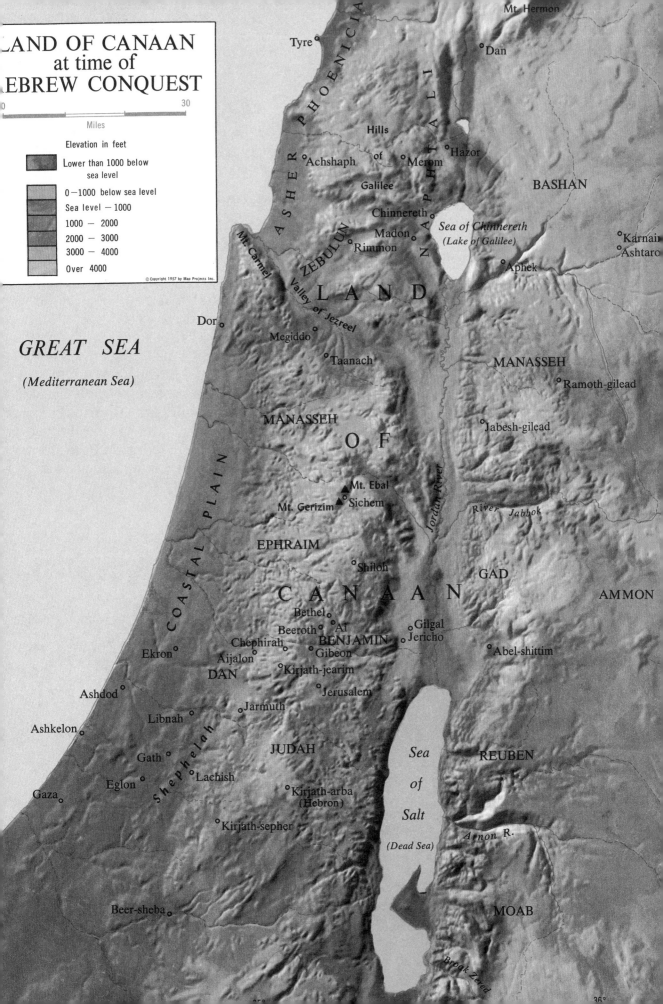

LAND OF CANAAN at time of EBREW CONQUEST

0   30
Miles

Elevation in feet

Lower than 1000 below sea level
0 – 1000 below sea level
Sea level – 1000
1000 – 2000
2000 – 3000
3000 – 4000
Over 4000

© Copyright 1957 by Map Projects Inc.

GREAT SEA

(Mediterranean Sea)

Mt Hermon

Tyre

PHOENICIA

Dan

Hills of Galilee

Achshaph

Merom

Hazor

BASHAN

Chinnereth

Sea of Chinnereth (Lake of Galilee)

ZEBULUN

Madon

Rimmon

NAPHTALI

Karnai

Ashtaro

Aphek

ASHER

Mt. Carmel

Valley of Jezreel

L A N D

Dor

Megiddo

Taanach

MANASSEH

Ramoth-gilead

Jabesh-gilead

MANASSEH

O F

Mt. Ebal

Mt. Gerizim

Sichem

Jordan River

River Jabbok

EPHRAIM

Shiloh

GAD

AMMON

C A N A A N

COASTAL PLAIN

Bethel

Beeroth

Ai

BENJAMIN

Gibeon

Gilgal

Jericho

Chephirah

Abel-shittim

Ekron

Aijalon

Kirjath-jearim

DAN

Jerusalem

Ashdod

Jarmuth

Libnah

Ashkelon

Shephelah

JUDAH

Sea of Salt

REUBEN

Gath

Eglon

Lachish

Kirjath-arba (Hebron)

Gaza

Kirjath-sepher

(Dead Sea)

Arnon R.

Beer-sheba

MOAB

Brook Zered

36°

were waiting at the edge of the field during the reaping, to glean in the fields. They picked up the remaining stalks, together with any grain that had fallen to the ground. Often farmers left stalks for gleaning in troublesome corners of their fields.

By Moses' law, farmers were told to reap only once. They were not to return to their fields for grain that had been overlooked. They were to follow the same rule in olive orchards and vineyards. Any produce that remained was for gleaning by strangers, orphans, and widows. The reason given was this: "Remember that you were a slave in Egypt" (Deut. 24).

"An inheritance for your tribes" (p. 279)

The land of Canaan was divided among the Twelve Tribes of Israel, with the tribes of Joseph's sons Ephraim and Manasseh receiving what would have been his share. The Levites were priests and had no land. (See map.)

Jericho (p. 268)

Jericho was the first city Joshua attacked in his campaign to win the land of Canaan for the Hebrews. This city is the most ancient dwelling place in the Holy Land. The first town on that site was built around 6000 B.C., and people still live there today.

Jericho was known in Bible times for its rich harvests of grain and fruit, and for its luxuriant palms. In fact, it was commonly called "the city of palm trees." Jericho was such a flourishing city because it had a good supply of excellent water from springs in the nearby hills.

Cities in the land of Canaan were usually surrounded by walls.

314

Judges (p. 282)

The people the Bible calls judges were not judges as we know them today, but were self-appointed leaders in times of trouble. These heroes and heroines led the Israelites against their enemies.

During the times of the judges, the Israelites had won a foothold in the Promised Land, but many Canaanite foes were still living there among them. In addition a new enemy, the Philistines (see Philistines), were proving especially troublesome.

Kenites (p. 282)

The Kenites were a clan of the tribe of Midianites. Zipporah, Moses' wife, and Jethro, Moses' father-in-law, were of the Kenites.

Midianites (p. 287)

The Midianites in the stories in this volume invaded Canaan from their home in Sinai.

Millstone (p. 291)

A millstone is a round, very heavy stone used to grind wheat or barley into flour, or to press oil from olives.

At home, women ground flour with a hand mill made of two small millstones, one set on top of the other. Each was about 18 inches in diameter. In the center of the top stone there was a small hole. Grain to be ground into flour was dropped into this hole. A wooden handle was used to turn the millstone and grind the flour. This was hard work and it usually took two women to turn the heavy stone. The women ground just enough flour for one day's baking.

Overlords (p. 296)

The masters who were above all other masters were called overlords. During Samson's time, the Philistines were the Israelites' overlords.

Parapet (p. 271)

A parapet was a low protective wall built around the edge of a roof, a balcony, a bridge, or other high place.

Parched grain (p. 306)

Parched grain, also called parched corn in the Bible, was grain that had been dried in the sun. It was used as a snack and could be carried unspoiled by travelers and soldiers for many weeks.

Philistines (p. 294)

The Philistines lived along the southern part of the coast of Canaan. They had invaded the area and were believed to have come from islands in the Mediterranean, so were known as "the peoples of the sea." The Philistines were extremely successful in Canaan because their land had excellent soil for farming. Before long, they became producers of rich crops of grain, fruits, and vegetables. The Philistines built five beautiful cities: Gaza, Ashdod, Ekron, Gath, and Ashkelon. (See Ashkelon.)

The Philistines and Israelites were constantly at war with each other. The iron industry developed by the Philistines supplied them with fine weapons and war chariots, and with these they were able to maintain superiority over the Israelites, who had not yet learned the secrets of iron-making.

"Raise up the name of the dead upon his inheritance" (p. 308)

According to a custom called Levirate marriage, a man was obliged to marry his brother's widow if the brother had left no sons. The sons resulting from the new marriage would inherit the dead man's property, as if they had been his own sons. If the dead man had no brothers, the nearest male relative was obliged to marry the widow.

Reapers (p. 305)

The people who reaped, or cut down, the ripened grain were called reapers. To cut the grain stalks, the reaper used a curved cutting tool called a scythe. When first invented, this instrument had a cutting blade made of flint, a hard dark stone. After people had learned metal-working, the blade of the scythe was made of bronze, and later, of iron.

The reaper grasped a handful of grain stalks and cut them off with his scythe. These he tied together with a piece of straw to make a sheaf, or bundle. The sheaves were stacked in the field to be carried off for threshing.

Shekels (p. 288)

A shekel was a measure of weight, as are our ounce, gram, and pound. There were no coins or paper money used in the land of Canaan at this time, so wealth was measured in terms of shekels of gold. Thus, if something was worth 200 shekels of gold, it was worth a lump of gold that weighed 200 shekels. Such lumps of gold were used to purchase costly articles and land.

Most purchases in those days were made by barter, or exchange. If one man wanted an item owned by another, he would find something of equal value to exchange, thus trading by barter.

Although prices were quoted in shekels, a coin called a shekel did not appear until hundreds of years later and then it was made of silver. The Israelites never made coins of gold.

Tob (p. 292)

The land of Tob was an area to the east of the Sea of Chinnereth, now known as the Sea of Galilee.

Trumpets of rams' horns (p. 273)

The Israelites made trumpets from the curved horns of male sheep, called rams. The horns were straightened out by being heated, and sounded a single note when they were blown into. They were used on religious occasions and to call men to battle.

The Hebrews also used silver trumpets that were first made by Israelite silversmiths at the request of Moses. They were used to summon people to religious services and other events. Today a ram's-horn trumpet is called a shofar and is used during some Jewish religious celebrations.

Wineskins (p. 277)

In biblical times, wine was stored and sometimes carried in a vessel called a wineskin, which was made from a tanned animal skin. The skin of an ox could hold many gallons of wine. A goatskin held much less.

Before the wine was poured into the tanned skins, they were greased to keep the wine from seeping out.

Goatskins were also used to carry water and milk. Milk was churned into butter in a goatskin container.

Winnowing (p. 307)

Winnowing is the process of cleaning grain of straw and chaff. After grain has been threshed, or separated from the stalks, it is still mixed with chaff, bits of husk, small leaves, and stems. To clear these away, the Israelites threw the threshed wheat or barley up into the air with special wooden forks and shovels. As the breeze blew through the grain, the light chaff and straw were carried away by the wind, but the heavier grain fell to the ground.

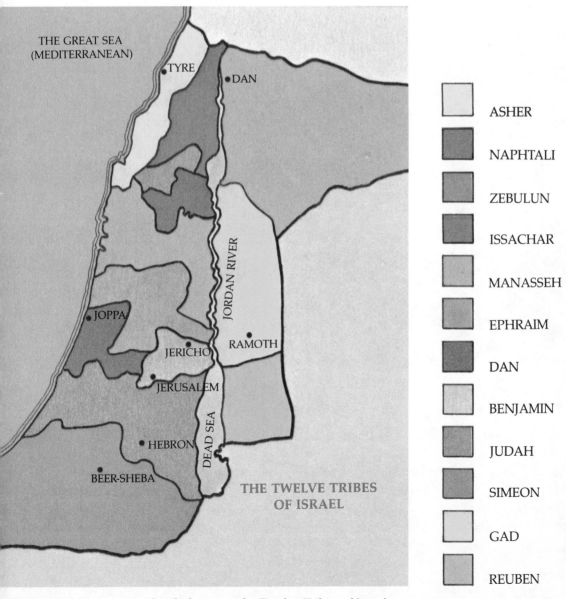

THE GREAT SEA (MEDITERRANEAN)

TYRE

DAN

JORDAN RIVER

JOPPA

JERICHO

RAMOTH

JERUSALEM

DEAD SEA

HEBRON

BEER-SHEBA

THE TWELVE TRIBES OF ISRAEL

ASHER

NAPHTALI

ZEBULUN

ISSACHAR

MANASSEH

EPHRAIM

DAN

BENJAMIN

JUDAH

SIMEON

GAD

REUBEN

The land of Canaan was divided among the Twelve Tribes of Israel.